ALDERSHOT & DISTRICT
TRACTION Co LTD

1906—ANNIVERSARY
SOUVENIR BOOK

Compiled by Malcolm John

JOHN HALLEWELL PUBLICATIONS

Published by John Hallewell Publications
Hallewell House, 38 High Street, Chatham, Kent
ISBN 0905540 63 8

First published 1981
© Malcolm John 1981

Designed and produced by Chambers Green Limited, Tunbridge Wells
Printed in Great Britain by R. J. Acford Limited, Chichester

This is our second 'Souvenir Book' in our growing range of transport books. This collection of photographs, memories, cuttings has not been easy to compile as selecting from the large amounts of material sent in by the families of former employees, the archives of the Company and of Messrs Hestair Dennis of Guildford, has been by a process of deduction according to reproduction quality and event importance. It has also prompted me to consider a longer account of the fascinating story of buses in this area.

The old 'Traco' company had an affinity with its passengers and staff, in those days when our present financial and traffic difficulties seemed farther away and when the livery of a company was as important as the names on trains.

Re-live those days and travel with us through the lanes of nostalgia with the Aldershot and District Traction Co Ltd.

Special thanks for help in producing this book go to Mr Bruce Tidy, the Press Officer for Alder Valley, Mr Malcolm Chase, also of Alder Valley, Peter Stonham of NBC Press Department, and to Bob Loveland of Hestair Dennis Ltd.

MALCOLM JOHN

Coach outing to Bognor 1951.

It was 75 years ago that omnibuses first carried passengers around the rural lanes of Surrey and Hampshire. Four Miles-Daimler 20 hp double deck buses were purchased from the Hastings and St Leonards Motor Omnibus Co Ltd, running every half hour between Aldershot and Farnborough for a fare of 3d. This operation was titled the 'Aldershot and Farnborough Motor Omnibus Company'. Services gradually expanded and in 1912 the Aldershot and District was formed with the original workings and vehicles as a new company. The routes were extended as far as Farnham and Camberley. Its opening aims were to carry out the business of operators of omnibuses, carriers of goods and acquiring the Aldershot and Farnborough Motor Omnibus Company Ltd. It also took over vehicles operating to Farnham and Haslemere. The twenties and thirties saw rapid expansion in the company's operations and vehicles, from under a hundred in 1924 to some 250 in the early thirties, including 42 double decks (21 with covered tops), 160 single decks, 15 charabancs and some 20 saloon coaches. In 1930 the capital of the company was £200,000 with the Southern Railway as a shareholder, in order to regularise the relationship with the Railways Board. The Head Office was always at Halimote Road in Aldershot and there were outstations at Guildford, Haslemere and Woking.

The Aldershot and District Company had from its start an affinity with Dennis vehicles based locally at Guildford. Indeed a large selection of Dennis vehicles is depicted in this volume. From the uncomfortable solid tyred open charabancs of the late twenties to the Lolines of the sixties, the duo-tone Lancets, Lances, Falcons graced the area and carried countless thousands to such events as the Aldershot Tattoo and the Farnborough Air Displays. At the height of the shows' popularity there was a bus leaving Aldershot every thirty seconds in the early fifties. During the troubled war years large numbers of troops were conveyed by the company, Aldershot being a principal military area.

It is also interesting to note that the company had an interest in conveying goods as well as passengers for there were several steam wagons (Fodens) in the fleet (20 in 1914), and they were still carrying goods (albeit by bus) in the 1930s in conjunction with the Southern Railway.

So by the time of the Silver Jubilee of the company the stock had increased dramatically from the initial four to several hundred, the passengers carried up from ¾ million to 20 million, a network of routes stretching as far as Reading and Egham in the north (and then by express to London), Horsham in the east, Bognor Regis by express to the south and Winchester to the south west.

It would of course be interesting to check the growth of passenger traffic to the present moment as the whole industry is suffering from economies and recession, but there has been a drop since the top in the fifties of some 52 million. Since the umbrella operations of the National Bus Company (A & District joining with Thames Valley Traction to become Alder Valley) in the early seventies there has been a compression of services and closing of garages, as well as the demise of the distinctive company livery, vanishing into history. Still perhaps the current interest by the NBC and its constituent companies in repainting some vehicles into 'special birthday livery' to mark anniversaries, etc., might spread to the regeneration of individual company livery and company identity.

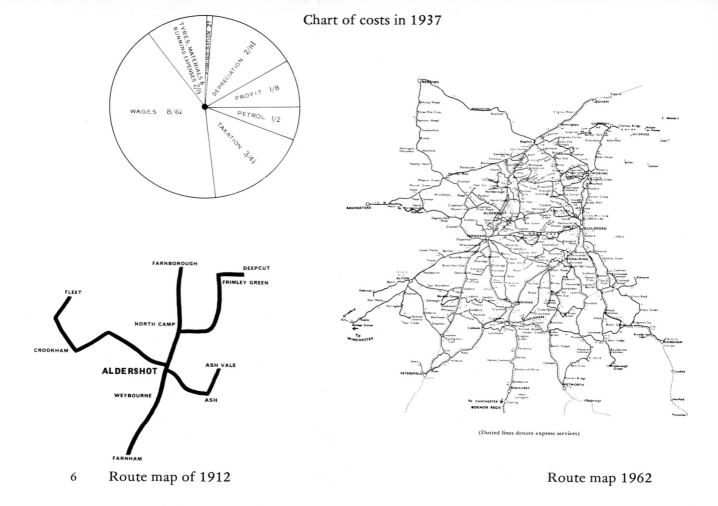

Chart of costs in 1937

TYRES, MATERIALS &
RUNNING EXPENSES 2/1½
INSURANCE 2½

DEPRECIATION 2/11¾

WAGES 8/6¼

PROFIT 1/8

PETROL 1/2

TAXATION 3/4½

FLEET

CROOKHAM

FARNBOROUGH

NORTH CAMP

ALDERSHOT

WEYBOURNE

FARNHAM

DEEPCUT

FRIMLEY GREEN

ASH VALE

ASH

6   Route map of 1912

(Dotted lines denote express services)

Route map 1962

ALDERSHOT'S LUXURY COACHES

NEW TYPE ON LONDON EXPRESS SERVICE.

To-day (Friday) there is being put on the road by the Aldershot and District Traction Co. the latest development in road coach travel.

The vast strides made by the road transport industry in recent years has left one wondering whether anything more can possibly be done for the comfort of the travelling public.

These latest coaches, which are being put on the London express service by the Aldershot and District Traction Co., Ltd., prove that human ingenuity and skill are still being applied to the problem, and Aldershot can now boast of a coach service which for comfort and coziness is second to none.

Everything possible appears to have been done in the interests of passengers. The seating accommodation has been entirely redesigned to the Company's own specifications. The seats are in pairs on either side of a central gangway, but the inner (or gangway) seat of each pair is a few inches in front of its neighbour, so that the passenger nearest the window does not obscure the view of the person seated beside him or her. On the gangway side each seat is provided with an arm rest. The seats are designed to fit every part of the back, and are provided with shoulder rests of sponge rubber, giving feather-pillow comfort to the neck and back of the head. Extra knee space is provided, and there is ample room for passengers to place their feet under the seat in front of them. All seats face the front of the coach.

The coach is lighted by electricity. There is individual lighting for each seat, and the lights are so placed that passengers can read in comfort while travelling. Each light is controlled by a separate switch, which can be operated by the passengers. A bell push is also within the reach of every passenger.

Ash trays and rug rails and a floor covering of thick fibre are among other amenities of this new type of coach, which is so commodious that a 6ft. person can stand upright without hitting the roof.

Heating is provided by means of a system of hot-water pipes inside the coach, operated by the driver, the modern system of ventilation enables fresh air to get into the vehicle without the creation of draughts, the windows are provided with winding handles, which can be operated by the passengers, and are fitted with exterior louvres.

Ample luggage accommodation is provided by a rack big enough to take a full sized suitcase, thus avoiding the necessity for passengers to "nurse" their bags and parcels.

The upholstery and general decoration of the interior harmonize beautifully, the colour scheme being a soft, restful combination of grey and black.

The modern low-slung body is fitted on an improved chassis, from which vibration has been entirely eliminated. This is done by the use of efficient shock absorbers and the latest balloon low-pressure tyres. These new coaches are so admirably designed that they run with the smoothness of a limousine motor car.

Twelve of these coaches are being put on the London service from to-day (Friday).

The coaches they are replacing will be put on the daily service to the coast from Aldershot, Farnborough, Camberley, and Fleet, and will also be available for private parties for any desired destination.

Photo by Gale & Polden, Ltd., Aldershot.

THE INTERIOR OF THE NEW COACH.

THEY NEVER DIE

WONDERS WITH WORN-OUT BUSES

Where do the buses go in the winter time of their lives? is a question many are asking to-day, when it is well known that to ask for a spare tyre is like asking for the moon—let alone a spare 48-seater bus. The enquiring layman need go no further than the Halimote Road headquarters of the Aldershot and District Traction Company to find the answer. Here he will learn that old buses never die, and they do not, in fact, even fade away.

There is practically nothing the Aldershot and District Company cannot do with tired and worn-out buses. The swift attention of their engineers, smiths, bodywork specialists, and upholstery repair department can turn a worn-out vehicle into as good as new in these days when "make do and mend" applies to public interest as much as to anything else.

Foreman Henry Redrup, of 3, Christmas Place Aldershot, who has been with the Company thirty-eight years, always reckons to have six or seven buses in his bodyshop. "They have been overworked all through the war, and we're now carrying more passengers than pre-war with the same number of buses," says he. "No wonder the poor things have to be given refresher treatment every so often.

"There's one in here at the moment for which we are making a complete new body, all but for the roof. Before the war some of the buses would have been scrapped and replaced with new ones, but now we can't get them, so we have to make the old ones as good as new."

And this, Arthur Coyne, the charge hand, and his men do, ably helped by the men in all the other departments of the Aldershot "hospital for tired buses." Sheet metal is short, material for upholstered seats is short, everything but a cheerful spirit and will to overcome all such difficulties is short. And so the men of the repair department keep on sending back to the busy transport front revived, rejuvenated buses, to continue their task of carrying passengers in comfort and with speed.

They don't reckon to let anything stand in their way when they set out to restore a flagging bus, not even lack of materials. Outside the bodyshop, for instance, there lies the trunk of an oak tree cut down from the Company's sports ground where it was getting in the way. One day soon the sports ground oak will be playing its part in carrying passengers from Woking to Weybridge, or from Alton to Aldershot Town.

That is the spirit of the men who repair your buses, the "back room boys" of the bus routes who play as big a part as any in providing the regular and unfailing service which has become accepted just as a matter of course.

NEW 'BUSES FOR OLD.—'Buses are now again everybody's form of transport, but there will be few extra vehicles to carry the thousands of erstwhile owner-drivers. Even more work will devolve on the department of the Aldershot & District Traction Co. which takes old and damaged 'buses, reconditions them and returns them to service, smart and road-worthy. Picture shows the foreman, Mr. Henry Redrup, and members of his team of "beauty specialists," at work on their task of rejuvenation.

Damage done to an Aldershot bus in a collision with a London-bound bus at Lavant, near Chichester. Ten people were taken to hospital.

WOKING BUS WARFARE.

COUNCIL AND ALDERSHOT CO.'S UNAUTHORISED SERVICE.

THREAT TO REFUSE ALL LICENSES.

Another stage was reached on Tuesday evening, at the meeting of the Woking Council, in the bus warfare which is proceeding in the district at the present time, and as was exclusively reported in our issue of three weeks ago.

It will be recalled that we then stated that following the refusal of the Council to grant the Aldershot Traction Co. permission to operate a service from the Grand Theatre to Chertsey, via the Six Cross Roads, and The Bleak, and the refusal of the Council to recognise the claim of the Company to a monopoly over the route, the Aldershot Co. threatened to "flood the streets of Woking" with buses, and to put a bus in front of every one of Messrs. Fox's buses.

The view was taken at the time that it was a "game of bluff," but at the meeting of the Omnibus Committee on Monday week the Omnibus Inspector reported that on August 16 the Aldershot Co. had put an unauthorised service into operation on the Woking-Chertsey route via Six Cross Roads, and further that the same company had commenced a revised service on the Woking-Sunningdale and Camberley (via Chobham and Windlesham) route just in front of Messrs. Fox's service, without waiting for the sanction of the "Through" Joint Advisory Committee.

After considering the report of the Inspector, and a letter of protest from Messrs. Fox & Sons regarding the Woking-Chertsey service, the Omnibus Sub-Committee instructed the Clerk of the Council to ask the Aldershot and District Traction Co. to discontinue the service *forthwith*, and to inform them that unless this was done the Council, at their meeting on October 8, would be recommended not to renew licenses in respect of *any* of their vehicles."

With respect to the Woking and Camberley service, it was reported that the Windlesham Council had disapproved of the Aldershot Co.'s proposal and the Woking Omnibus Committee recommended that consideration of the matter be postponed until after the next meeting of the Joint Advisory Committee.

"THE BUS WARFARE."

In initiating the discussion at the Council meeting, Cllr. Quartermaine said he hoped the Council was taking note of the seriousness of the position. When last mentioned, he did not think that the threat of the Aldershot Company would materialise. Unfortunately, that had happened, however, and the Company had commenced to run the unauthorised service. It seemed by this that a challenge had been issued as to the right of local authorities to allocate the way the bus services should be run. If that sort of thing were allowed to continue the work of the Omnibus Sub-Committee would be brought to nought, and chaos would result.

He brought the point up because of its far-reaching effects. He had no doubt that the Company would make a test case regarding the point in question. The Council would be called upon to carry out their threats with regard to the discontinuation of the licensing of buses, and he hoped that he, as Chairman of the Omnibus Sub-Committee, would have the support of the Council in the matter.

The Clerk read the correspondence he had had with the Aldershot Co., which was briefly to the effect that the Company did not propose to discontinue the service. The "Through" Omnibus Joint Advisory Committee, he explained, had unanimously approved the action of the Sub-Committee, and had instructed him to write and acquaint the authorities with the steps the Council were going to take, and to ask for their support in the matter.

SUGGESTED REFUSAL OF LICENSES.

After Cllr. Whitburn had expressed his view, Cllr. Campbell asked whether the Council had to wait until the time came for the renewal of the licenses, or whether some steps could not be taken before that date. Would it not be possible to refuse the licenses for 9 drivers and 8 conductors applied for by the Aldershot Co.; undoubtedly they would be used on the new service?

Cllr. Jackman suggested that the police should be notified that an unauthorised bus service, and one endangering public life, was being run in Woking.

Cllr. Renshaw said that trouble between the local bus companies and the Aldershot Traction Co. had been going on for some time. On this route the Council must hold their own, for the trouble had been going on long enough and should be brought to an end.

Cllr. Briant, agreeing, stated that if the Aldershot Co. had its own way in the case, all the other companies would want to do the same, and there would be no end of trouble.

Cllr. Campbell said the Aldershot Co. wrote notifying them that they were going to run an unauthorised service, and then asked the Council to grant them licenses for new men. It would not be hard on the men if the licenses were not granted, but would have the same effect in that respect as the stoppage of the unauthorised service.

It was finally decided to grant the drivers' and conductors' licenses until Oct. 8, when the licenses for the buses again came up for renewal, and when the Council will decide what steps they will take to deal with the action of the Aldershot Company.

COMFORT FOR BUS PASSENGERS.

NEW AND LUXURIOUS BUS.

The Aldershot and District Traction Company are to be congratulated on the luxurious form of travelling they have provided for passengers. The new type of bus, which was put into service a few days ago, appears to be the last thing in comfort and luxuriousness, and an *Aldershot News* representative who made the first journey in one of these vehicles, heard many favourable comments from delighted passengers, one of whom described it as first-class travel at third-class rate.

The chassis is the Dennis low load line E type, fitted with a 40 h.p. engine. The body is longer than in the older type of single-decker bus, and the arrangement of the seats gives an impression of greater width. The seats are of the semi-bucket type, and are fitted with spring backs, which afford an unusual degree of comfort.

JOURNEY IN COMFORT.

The springing of the seats and of the vehicle itself is so efficient that the bus is every bit as comfortable as an ordinary pleasure motor-car, and one can imagine passengers taking long journeys in one of these vehicles without feeling at all tired. The front of the bus is somewhat after the style of the London buses, the driver being seated alongside the engine. Another advantage is the provision of only two steps, which is a great help in alighting from and boarding these buses.

The body, which is by Stracker and Brown, is fitted with roll-top shutters, and all the windows are of the drop pattern, and the bus can be turned in two minutes from a closed saloon—for that is the impression it gives—into an open coach.

The bus runs on big pneumatic tyres, 38 x 7, the front wheels having single tyres and the rear wheels twin tyres. All the wheels are detachable, and a spare wheel is carried in case of punctures.

COMPLETE SAFETY.

But the finest feature of this new type of bus is the braking system, which is so efficient that passengers need have no qualms when the vehicle descends even the steepest hill. Four wheel brakes are fitted on the Servo braking system. The function of the Servo gear is to augment, by means of mechanical power, the effort of the driver when applying the brakes. This mechanical power is provided by means of a single plate dry clutch driven from the gear-box, and is applied to the front and rear wheels by depressing the foot-brake pedal. This is the same braking system that is fitted to the Rolls-Royce cars.

Its efficiency was demonstrated to our representative on a straight stretch of road at Hindhead. The driver—who, by the way, appeared to be proud of his new bus —accelerated until his speedometer recorded 28 miles per hour. Then he applied the foot-brake. Instantly the pace slackened, and the bus pulled up almost dead within little more than its own length, as smoothly as if it had been pulled up by a violent gust of wind.

When the travelling public use this new type of bus they will undoubtedly want more of them, and what is more they will want them on every route.

It may be of interest to add that the Company's buses cover 400,000 miles per month, and that the number of buses in use is now 175—an increase of 75 per cent. as compared with two years ago. Many of the new types of bus are quite comfortable, but none of them give the comfort of the

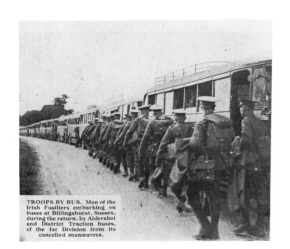

TROOPS BY BUS. Men of the
Irish Fusiliers embarking on
buses at Billingshurst, Sussex,
during the return, by Aldershot
and District Traction buses,
of the 1st Division from its
cancelled manœuvres.

ALDERSHOT 'BUS ROUTE DEVELOPMENTS: Clearing the way for the double deck
'buses, which will be running next year between Aldershot and Winchester.

A very familiar shot of the first charabanc owned by the Aldershot and Farnborough Motor Omnibus Company Ltd. The person, equally well known, was Mr Jim Hunt who served the firm for more than fifty years and is seen here as conductor for the 1910 outing from the Wellington Works at the Grove, Aldershot.

One of the first 'Leylands' in the fleet with driver and conductor en route to Aldershot Station. No proper documentation exists with regard to these early Leylands except for some registration numbers: AA 5163, AA 5162, AA 5070, and AA 5042(?). Note the front headlamps carried at the level of the driver's cab roof.

A fine view of an early 1919 Dennis 'Subsidy' bus with possibly an original Brush body, replaced in 1920 by an Aldershot and District 26 seater charabanc body.

An interesting side elevation of an early Dennis bus operated by Aldershot and District prior to the use of their scroll emblem. The solid tyres, battery box, starting handle and open driver's cockpit can be easily distinguished. There is a problem over dating, however, for there were no Dennis buses in the fleet until 1919 yet this view was captioned as being both 1914 and 1918 in other sources.

The Dennis SOS was a compact 30 seater bus carrying Strachan and Brown coachwork. The typical exterior ladder to the luggage rack and the large oval rear window can be seen clearly. The rather ungainly entrance belies its earlier 1923/4 origins. Note the solid wheel centres at the front. It took its last journey for A&D in 1936 when it was sold to King and Taylor of Gloucester.

This A&D coach is decorated for the Aldershot Carnival in 1929 and includes several poems and advertisements for the company. The vehicle shown is a 1923 Daimler Y (HO 6208) with a 34 seater bus body. It saw service for only a few years being withdrawn later in the carnival year to C. Bruce of Hammersmith.

A bodybuilder's photograph of a 1924 Dennis is HO 6268, with its 36 seats. It remained in service until being sold in 1930 to 'King and Taylor' of Godalming. The coachlines are a pleasing feature of this early vehicle as are the 'ships wheel' type of road wheels sporting Dunlop tyres.

18

This view has been inserted to show minor period details such as the motor horn, the front destination board, split screen with pivoting window, minuscule headlights and large seat hooks behind equally large window openings — the whole bus weighing under 3 tons.

Looking really more like an early minibus was this late twenties Dennis G. Note the rather ugly front doorway and the saloon car type raked windscreen. The seats look thin and very uncomfortable for all but the shortest journeys.

An interior view of a late twenties Dennis coach with covered seats and netted luggage racks and internal wood surrounds.

OU 1117 was new in 1929 being a Dennis EV/Dennis B32. It remained in service until 1937 when it was sold to Dawson of London.

22

A splendid full frontal view of the Dennis of 1929 showing the suspension and very thin tyres used at this time. The starting handle may also be observed.

A side view of another 1929 bus of Dennis/Strachan construction. This one was
OU 1103 a 31 seater which was withdrawn in 1936 and sold to Stokes of Overton.

24

A double deck Dennis H with Strachan 48 seater bodywork of 1929 clearly showing its external rear staircase, rear platform with running board and all square bodywork. Eight years later it was sold to J. Clark of London.

One of the six Dennis 'F' types purchased by A&District in 1928. These had 28 seater Strachan bodywork, charabanc style with folding hoods and were converted to forward control in 1932 and given 30 seater bus bodies. This view shows OT 8284 entering service in 1929. This vehicle was withdrawn in 1940 and sent to the War Department.

This was one of the five 20 seater Gilfords with Strachan and Brown bodies purchased in 1928. It was obviously intended for luxury travel having curtains throughout and a covered luggage rack. They were withdrawn in 1930 and all passed to the East Kent Road Car Co, no doubt due to the thinning out arrangement with British Railways.

OU 1112 was a 1929 Dennis E double decker of 48 seater capacity (Hall Lewis body). The styling of the Hall Lewis was always distinctive with the sharply raking windscreen, the projecting front curtain and the open siderails. After eight years it was withdrawn passing to Vale Motor Works of Surbiton.

Another side view of a 1929 double deck bus is OU 1113, a Dennis H with Hall Lewis bodywork and 48 seats. The front overhang can now be clearly seen as can the maximum use of advertising space on the stair treads! On withdrawal it too passed to Vale Motor Works.

A 1930 Dennis HV carrying Strachan 48 seater coachwork. The vehicle standing at the Dennis Factory at Guildford was OU 6844 and was withdrawn in 1937 to Clarks of London. We can note the raised speed limit of 20 mph!

A close up of the 1932 single liveried Dennis Lancet/Strachan B32. With the outbreak of war it was requisitioned in 1940 by the War Department. This was the first Lancet in the A&District fleet having 16'4" wheelbase, 4 cylinder petrol engine and having the heavy charabanc type radiator to cool the 30 hp engine.

One of a batch of eight Dennis Lancets with 30 seater coach bodywork by Strachans was CG 9598, new in 1935. It was withdrawn in 1949 and sold to M. Hill of Hayling Island. It is seen here converted to an ambulance in drab wartime type livery. The express coach service can still be clearly seen along the window edges.

Converted to a tree lopper in 1948 was ex CCG 334 (new in 1937), a Dennis Lance. Carrying fleet number 16 this view also shows the use of trade plates 351 HO. The original body was a Strachan 48 seater double decker bus. It was finally withdrawn from service in 1958 and sold to Bakers of Dorking.

Carrying patriotism to the extreme a loyal Coronation coach of 1937, a brand new Dennis Lancet 2 with Strachan 32 seater bus body. In 1940 it was sent to the War Department and in 1951 it was disposed of to J. Brown of Feltham.

34

A 1937 Dennis Lance with a Strachan 48 seater body was CCG 329 shown here in rather drab plain livery. It was scrapped in 1950 and the body sold.

However, this Dennis Lancet 2 with its luxury bodywork shows British bodybuilding at its best, from the route splayed out along the roof line, the curtained windows, the company scroll and different wheel hubs. It was new in 1938 having 32 seater bodywork and served in the fleet until 1954, passing then to Jones of Chertsey.

One of the two rare appearances of Leyland in the fleet was a TD7 with 48 seater East Lancs bodywork. Lasting in service until 1958, this 1942 Leyland was pleasingly different to the few Guys and the large stocks of Dennis buses. On disposal they passed to PVD (Export) of Rugby.

An equally rare glimpse of one of the few Guys to appear in the fleet in 1944. Looking very smart in its two tone livery and new Weymann body (1950) with the clock at Guildford behind. The bus accommodated 51 passengers more than in the original Roe body. After 18 years of service it passed to Vokes Engineers of Guildford and was used as a staff bus.

Dating from the end of the war was EOT 28, a 1945 Guy Arab II with its second body a lowbridge East Lancs 56 seater, replacing an earlier 48 seater Strachan. A feature of the bodywork was the rounded destination boxes.

Also new at the end of the war was EOT 30 a Guy Arab II which shows the original Strachan 48 seater bodywork. It was replaced in 1954 by an East Lancs 56 seater body. Compare this austere looking vehicle with the last view in dual tone livery. The extra long driver's window is worth noting as are the small windows with numerous openings and the square route box.

40

A 1940's Guy Arab II with its second (1950) body by Weymann seen here in a busy street scene in Guildford in the early fifties. The Austin A30, Wolseley and Morris Minor van also indicate the body styling of the period. These Guys carried 48 passengers for many of Aldershot and District double deckers were of low capacity. The prominent radiator is also interesting.

A fine photograph of a 1947 32 seater Dennis Lancet bus with the usual Strachan body-work. Compare the contour lines of the bus with COR 159, the latter having stylish radiator, mudguards, and rounded rear doorway. Its relatively short nine year service life meant that then it passed to the Dorking firm of E. J. Baker.

Showing the rear quarter of an Aldershot and District coach in London traffic in 1915 is GAA 609. It was a 1948 Dennis Lancet 32 seater vehicle and a company employee can just be seen at the back of the coach. It was withdrawn in 1961 and had several owners finally reaching Alscot motors in June 1962.

In usual A & District livery is GOU 833, a 1949 (entering service in 1950) Dennis Lance with pleasing East Lancs 57 seater bodywork. The split type destination box is worth noting. This batch of post war Lances, standard orders for A & District numbered some 23 buses. 833 was withdrawn in 1962 and sold to Margo of Addiscombe.

44

The needs for a small 20 seater bus in the early fifties were met by the Dennis Falcons. Shown here is GOU 850 an all Dennis product. These buses had pleasant lines with projecting bonnets similar to the small Guys of London Transport.

One of the two demonstrators built by Dennis Brothers was the 41 seater Strachan bus bodied Dennis Dominant. This vehicle, the second, arrived in 1951 and this was the first time that Dennis had opted for the underfloored engined single decker. A turbo charged version was also offered producing some 130 bhp. The styling looks complicated with dual 'stressed' wheel arches and an unusual ¾ sliding entry door. It lasted until 1966.

A most unusual vehicle was this single decker 41 seater Guy Arab bus. Not noted for 'single deck' use for the home market this one had East Lancs bodywork with very high waistline and sliding rear entrance. It was new in 1953 and the only one of its type in the Aldershot fleet.

Fleet number 200 carried on LAA 235 was a 1953 Dennis Lancet, with 38 seater coach body built by Strachans. This period saw the zenith of coachbuilding with stylish coachlines in sweeping arcs, before the introduction of all square box coaches. This view shows the Company stand at Rushmoor in August 1953. The destination blind tells us that this would be used for plying between Farnham and London on express work. However, in 1961 it was rebuilt to dual purpose standards having 38 seater bodywork and lasting until 1963 and being sold to a Surrey contractor.

An East Lancs Coachbuilder's photograph shows one of a batch of Dennis K4 Lances which arrived in the A&D fleet in 1954 and very smart it looks. The lowbridge body with the side gangway can clearly be seen on the upper deck. Most of these buses were withdrawn in 1964-5.

An interesting view of the rather ungainly rear end of the 1954 Dennis Lance with East Lancs 56 seater body. The vehicle appears to be excessively wide and this is not helped by the curved and rounded window and body styling. After a short ten year life it was withdrawn and sold to Essex dealers and on to Pilchers of Chatham.

Another Dennis Falcon with not so common Strachan 30 seater bus body was LOU 66. New in 1954, it was one of a batch of 23 delivered. It was a lightweight vehicle with a choice of normal or forward control versions and two engines, later two more, until in 1952 the 5½ litre diesel and 5 speed box were most common as standard equipment.

An unusually wintery scene for the south of England shows an AEC Reliance (RCG 602) with Weymann bodywork, 43 seats and complete with minor snowfall! Just how far up the road at Millbridge, Frensham this bus got on the last day of December in 1961 we cannot say but it was probably further than the Lance in the inset.

The sixties saw widespread expansion of single deck coaching and new in 1962 was
466 FCG. It was an exhibit at the Park Royal stand at the 1962 Commercial Motor
Show. It was a 49 seater coach on an AEC Reliance chassis. The coach used on express
services depicts yet another variation of the A&D changing livery of the time.   53

Arriving at the same time as 466 FCG was another AEC Reliance with dual purpose 41 seater bodywork also by Park Royal. It, however, did not pass on to Alder Valley being withdrawn prior to 1972.

New in 1965 was another large batch of Dennis Lolines, the Mark III's. These had Weymann 68 seater bodies and have been a familiar sight in the fleet throughout the sixties and seventies. This photograph shows the last livery to be adopted by A&D prior to the new company in 1972. The Lolines now vanishing from the fleet were the last truly A&D double deck buses.

This 36' x 8' coach, mounted on an AEC Reliance chassis, one of five ordered by A&D had a 49 seater Metro-Cammell-Weymann body fitted. It became Alder Valley No 44 in 1972.

Three coaches also based on the AEC Reliance arrived in the same year as another change of livery for touring coaches, 1968, having stylish bodywork by Duple Northern but holding two less than the Willowbrook service buses designated dual purpose. The large windows and square styling was typical of the late sixties in coaching.

57

And finally, parked at Aldershot Bus Station in fleet number order are the 1968 AEC Reliances with dual purpose bodies holding 51 passengers, awaiting duties before the red paint brush of Alder Valley changed their identity as Aldershot and District buses for ever.

Showing that, as with many of the pioneer bus firms, Aldershot and District had some lorries, in this case steam lorries such as this 3 ton Foden, and in the inset view taken at Halimote Road are seven of the 20 in the fleet, with their operators in all their industrial splendour.

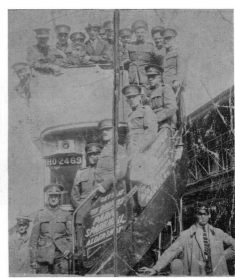

Two 1928 Dennis G 18 seater buses are neatly stored away in the new 1923 Alton Garage in the old fire station premises. OT 8597 was withdrawn in 1934 to King and Taylor and 8593 in 1940 to Arlington Motors. Also seen in Alton Depot is PF 2077, the 2½ ton Dennis with unknown 20 seater body acquired in 1928 from Tanners of Cobham. This lasted until 1932 when it went to Durnsfords of Newbury.

Note the uniforms and fashions in the third photograph, note, too, the driver smoking in this early shot taken in the thirties. Possibly the scarcest view in this book is the rare A&D bus with its complement of officers taken at the 1922 Derby. HO 2469 was Dennis Subsidy bus, 34 seater, open topped and with external rear staircase. This bus had two different bodies this one shown an Immuish Launch Co which remained until 1924 when a replacement 48 seater was added by Strachan and Brown. It was sold in 1930 to W. Smith Motors of London.

'K' Dept of RAE Farnborough on their day off on August 28th 1920. This splendid view clearly shows the 12 mph speed limit of this early charabanc, the driver's uniform and clothes of the period.

More day trippers sitting in the sun in an open topper of the late twenties, probably an
F type, with its canvas hood rolled back.

There was always plenty of support for sport and recreation from the company employees. They had a strong social club and a new meeting hall opened in the thirties. These views show the teams for the Bowls match (note the stake!) and the winners of the Darby Cup of 1922/3.

Production of this book would not have been possible without the assistance of the following for cuttings and photographs which were selected as follows.

Alder Valley Archives : 5, 12, 15, 16, 26, 29, 31, 32, 33, 36, 41, 42, 43, 46, 48, 49, 50, 52 and all other cuttings.

Michael Tidy : Front and rear covers.

Malcolm Chase : 28, 38, 39, 44, and via S. White, 35, 37, 45, 47, Vintage Press Society 17, 24, 25, (D. Jones) and J. Aston 40.

Dennis Brothers : Frontispiece, 18, 19, 20, 21, 22, 23, 30.
(Hestair Dennis Ltd)

Mr Redrup, Farnborough : 8, 34, 59 (inset), 63.

Mrs Jarvis, Farnborough : 3.

Mrs Strange, Aldershot : 60.

Mrs Palmer, Farnborough : 13, 62.

Mrs Carpenter : driver smoking 60.

Surrey Advertiser Picture Desk : 14.

If you have enjoyed this book then please send for our transport list.